THE VALVE

How the Body Opens When It Finally Feels Safe

Learning to Live Without the Weight

W. G. Vale

A body can only hold for so long.

Then it remembers how to open.

Your body is your oldest, wisest ally.

It learned to protect you before you had words for what it was protecting you from.

For years, many of us live braced for impact without knowing it.

We tighten around old pain. We hold our breath. We call this personality.

This is not a book about fixing yourself. This is a book about listening — to the intelligence that never stopped knowing.

When the valve opens, life flows.

Table of Contents

Part Four. The Opening

Part Five. Living Open

CODA

Before You Begin

This book is not meant to be rushed. It is something to return to, as different parts of you become ready.

I am not an authority here. I am a fellow traveler — someone who spent years not understanding what was happening inside himself, and then, slowly, imperfectly, began to see.

What you hold is not a system. It is not a prescription. It is a discovery, still unfolding, offered to you as companionship.

Read slowly. Feel as you go.

No one is behind. No one is late.

The valve opens when it opens.

This book is not a command. It is companionship.

There was a night I sat alone in my kitchen, long after the house had gone quiet.

The lights were still on, but I did not remember turning them on. A plate sat in front of me, untouched. I could not remember if I had eaten.

I had spent the day doing everything I was supposed to do. I had answered calls. I had solved problems. I had been useful. I had been needed.

From the outside, nothing was wrong.

And still — something in me would not move.

I sat there, hands resting on the table, staring at nothing I could name, with a feeling I had no language for.

Not sadness. Not anger. Not even exhaustion.

Just… a quiet pressure.

As if something inside me had been closing for years — and I had only just noticed I could no longer breathe the way I used to.

I did not call anyone. I did not reach for help.

I did what I had always done.

I stayed.

* * *

Before the Chair

A companion must first be a fellow traveler.

I did not arrive at this book as a teacher.

I arrived as the man at that table.

I came to this country as a boy from Ethiopia, carrying nothing the eye could count. I learned a new language one cold syllable at a time. I studied nursing in South Dakota, drove out to an Indian reservation, stood in the emergency rooms of Texas, bent over the bodies of the wounded in a Level 1 trauma bay in Houston — hands steady, mind narrowed to the single clean task in front of me. I trained as an anesthetist in Minnesota. I walked into operating rooms and held other people's breathing in my hands for twenty years. I was good at it. I was careful. I stayed.

I built a life the way a man builds a wall — brick by brick, each one set square, each one bearing the weight of the next. I married. I worked. I saved. Two sons arrived — Michael first, then Matthew — and the world rearranged itself around their small bodies the way a room rearranges around a fire.

I drove them to soccer practice. I sat on metal bleachers in the cold. I clapped for goals and I clapped, harder, for the misses — because a father learns quickly that a boy needs the clap more when he has failed than when he has won. I drove them to band practice. I sat in the parking lot with the engine running and a book on the dashboard. I drove them to tutors and to doctors and to the homes of friends whose names I tried to remember. I packed lunches at six in the morning. I stood in grocery store aisles deciding between the cereal they would eat and the cereal that was better for them and I chose, every time, the one they would eat. I worked nights. I worked weekends. I took call. I came home and I cooked and I cleaned and I listened and I tucked them in and I got up and I did it again.

This is not a complaint. This is a life. This is what a father does. I would do every hour of it again.

And both boys graduated. Both boys walked across the stage in a gown I had paid for and a cap I had straightened, and I sat in the audience and cried the particular tears a man cries when a long labor reaches the one thing it was aimed at. I had done it. We had done it.

And somewhere in all that building — somewhere between a late shift and a parent-teacher conference, between a birthday cake and a tax return — the marriage I had spent twenty-five years tending began, very quietly, to come apart.

It did not shatter. That would have been easier to explain. It fractured. The way a bone fractures when a body has been asked to carry, for too long, more than it was built to carry.

I will not tell you the details. They are not mine alone to tell. I will tell you only this: we ended it. After twenty-five years. And in the ending there was no villain, and there was no relief, and there was no story clean enough to hand to the people who would ask.

In my culture, a man does not divorce. A man endures. A marriage is not a contract you may dissolve; it is a covenant you are meant to carry to the grave. When the news reached my people, I watched their faces do the thing faces do when they are choosing between love and judgment. Some chose love. Some did not.

Later, when I met Colleen — when a second life began to rise, impossibly, from the first one — I remarried. I called the people I had grown up loving and I invited them to the wedding.

Some of them did not come.

They did not write. They did not call. They simply did not come. The silence of a people who have decided you are no longer quite who you were.

You fail at the one thing we agreed you would not fail at, and we remove our seat from your table.

I stood at that wedding in a suit I had chosen with care and I looked out at the empty chairs and I felt, for a moment, the full weight of what it costs to begin again inside a culture that does not forgive beginnings.

And still. I began.

I have run twenty marathons. I have crossed the finish line in Boston — the one every runner talks about, the one you do not qualify for by wanting to. I trained for it through a winter in which my body did what I asked of it, mile after mile, the long Saturday runs stretching into the pale dawn, the legs strong, the breath clean, the watch beeping its steady cadence. I was ready. I arrived. I ran. I finished. I wept on Boylston Street the way men weep when they have asked their body for something enormous and the body has said, quietly: yes.

I have also stood at mile two of a 5K — a 5K, three miles, a distance children run on a Saturday morning — and felt my legs refuse me. I have walked off the course with my hands on my hips and my lungs burning and my face hot with a shame no one else could see. Three miles. I have run Boston and I could not finish three miles. A stranger by the water station said, kindly, You are a good runner, I have seen you out here. And I could not look at him, because in that moment I did not feel like a runner. I felt like a fraud in expensive shoes.

I tell you all of this not because my life is unusual. I tell you because it is not.

Every person carries some version of it. The marriage that broke. The child who drifted. The parent who died before the last conversation. The body that betrayed you at mile two. The phone call that did not come. The wedding guest who stayed home. The culture that closed its door. The small, daily, unwitnessed labor of loving people and losing people and getting up again and again and again.

And inside all of it — under the soccer practices and the operating rooms and the fractured marriage and the finish lines and the empty chairs — something in me was closing. Not dramatically. Not all at once. A small valve, tightening by the year, tightening so slowly I called it by its other names: discipline, strength, professionalism, faith. I did not know, for a long time, that I was holding my breath. I did not know, for a long time, that a man can run a marathon and still not be breathing.

Until one night, in a kitchen, long after the house had gone quiet, I sat at a table I did not remember sitting down at, staring at a plate I did not remember preparing, and the body I had spent a lifetime not listening to finally said, without words: enough.

This book is what I found on the other side of that night.

I am not writing to you from a mountaintop. I am writing to you from the trail — a little further along, perhaps, than where you are standing now, but still on the same mountain, still walking, still, some mornings, unsure of the footing.

I have sat with the dying and I have sat with the dividing. I have held the hand of a man in a chair by a window, and I have also been the man at the kitchen table — unable, for a long time, to name what I was waiting for.

If I have anything to offer you, it is only this: I know the weight. I know the particular exhaustion of a life that looks, from the outside, like a life that is working. I know the shame of the unfinished 5K and the dignity of the finished marathon, and I know that the same man carries both. I know the lit kitchen at midnight. I know the plate that goes untouched.

I am not writing about you. I am writing beside you.

So before we go in to meet the man in the chair — and we will meet him, and he will change you, as he changed me — I wanted you to know who is walking beside you into that room.

A man who has built and broken and built again.

A father who drove to the practice and sat in the lot.

A husband who failed at one marriage and is working, daily, at another.

A runner who has finished Boston and walked off a 5K.

A son of a culture that did not always have a chair for him, and who learned, slowly, to pull up his own.

A man who sat, one night, at his own kitchen table, and finally heard what his body had been trying to tell him for years.

A fellow traveler. Nothing more. And nothing less.

Now. Let us go and meet him.

PART ONE

The Closed Valve

1

The Man in the Chair by the Window

The call came on a Tuesday.

A facility I sometimes consulted with had a resident they could no longer keep. Would I come and evaluate him?

I asked what the situation was.

There was a pause on the line. The pause a person takes when they are choosing between the honest answer and the professional one.

"We've run out of ideas," she said.

I told her I would come.

The drive there was ordinary. Small highway, low winter sky, the kind of morning that does not announce itself. I remember thinking about nothing in particular. I did not yet know that some of the most important meetings of a life arrive unannounced, wearing the clothes of a routine appointment.

When I pulled into the lot, a staff member was waiting at the door. Before I had my coat off, she began to tell me about him.

She was not unkind. She was tired. The particular tiredness of a person who has tried what they know how to try and found that none of it worked. Her sentences stacked like a case being built — the incidents, the behaviors, the medications that had not settled him, the placements that had not held. By the time she finished, she had handed me a thorough file on a man I had not yet seen.

I listened. I nodded when it was time to nod. And somewhere under the listening, a quieter thing was happening:

I was noticing how completely he had been replaced by his file.

When the staff finished, I asked if I could simply go in and sit with him for a while. No interview. No assessment forms. Just time.

She looked at me the way people look when you ask for something they did not know was available.

"Of course," she said.

They led me down a corridor that smelled of disinfectant and the indoor stillness of places that try to feel welcoming and never quite manage it. Fluorescent light. A radio somewhere playing something no one was listening to. The soft industrial hum of a building designed to hold human lives without ever quite touching them.

His door was open.

He was sitting in a chair by the window. The chair had been turned slightly, so he could face the light rather than the room. His hands rested in his lap — not folded, not clenched. Simply resting, the way hands rest when a person has stopped waiting for something.

He did not look up when I entered. Not because he hadn't noticed. Because he had learned, over a long time, that the people who came through that door rarely had anything for him that required his attention.

Gray hair, shorter on the sides than it wanted to be. A body that had carried illness for years — you could see it in the way he sat, the slight economy of movement that comes when the body learns to spend itself carefully. His face held a stillness that could have been mistaken for absence.

It was not absence. I saw that as soon as I sat down.

It was attention of a very particular kind. The attention of a person who has stopped expecting and has therefore become extraordinarily good at noticing.

I sat in the chair across from him. I did not take out a pen. I did not open a folder. I simply sat, and let the room be what it was.

He looked at me then.

Not to greet me. To read me. The way a person who has been misread a thousand times learns to read other people first — scanning for agenda, for conclusion, for the particular flavor of professional kindness that is almost always the prelude to being moved somewhere else.

He found none of it.

I had not come with a plan for him. I had come to meet him. In that room, on that ordinary Tuesday, this was the rarest thing.

Something in his face did not change, exactly — softened is too generous a word. But something in the *quality* of his stillness shifted. The way a room shifts when a window is opened and you do not yet know it has been opened; you only know the air is different.

We sat.

I do not remember who spoke first. I remember that nothing was rushed. I remember that the things he said, when he said them, came slowly — not because he was impaired, though the file had suggested he was, but because he had learned that most people did not wait long enough to let him finish a thought.

He had been, once, a man who worked with his hands. He had raised children, though he did not see them often now. He had lost his wife some years ago — he did not say how, and I did not ask. He had a condition that made his body unpredictable; there were days it obeyed him and days it did not. The world had steadily narrowed around him, the way worlds narrow around people whose bodies become inconvenient.

The facility was the third in four years.

He told me all of this without self-pity. In the same flat, careful register a person uses to read the weather report aloud to no one in particular.

And then, near the end of the hour, he said something I did not expect.

He said, "I used to garden."

I waited.

He said, "I had tomatoes. A row of them, along the fence. You had to tie them up with twine or they'd fall over under their own weight. You know how tomatoes are."

I nodded. He couldn't see the nod clearly, but he felt it — the way people feel a nod when someone is actually there.

He said, "I haven't touched dirt in six years."

He did not say it sadly. He said it the way you report a fact about a country you used to live in.

I sat with that for a long moment. Six years. A man who had once pressed his hands into soil and grown things that fed his family — hands that had not touched earth in six years, because the world had decided that men like him belonged indoors now, under fluorescent lights, their meals arriving on trays.

It was such a small loss. So small that no intake form would record it. And yet it contained the whole thing.

I did not offer him a garden. I did not make a promise I was not yet sure I could keep. I simply let his sentence stand between us, unhurried, and received it for what it was:

A man telling another man what he had lost, because for the first time in a long time someone was actually in the room.

After a while I said, "Would you tell me what else you miss?"

He looked at me again. Then, for the first time that morning, something that was almost a smile moved across the corner of his mouth. Not a smile of happiness. The smile of a man who has been asked a question he had stopped expecting anyone to ask.

He took a breath. He thought about it.

And then he began, slowly, to tell me.

I stayed with him much longer than the appointment required.

When I finally stood to go, he did not ask where I was going, or when I would be back, or whether I would take him with me. He had been asked too many times to hope for the answers other people give. He simply looked at me, and nodded once — the quiet, precise nod of a man acknowledging something real.

I nodded back.

At the door I paused. I do not know why. I turned, and I said the only thing I could honestly say:

"I'll come back."

He did not answer. He did not need to. His face held the quality of a person who had heard those words before from people who did not return, and who had nevertheless decided to believe me anyway — because hope, once it has been crushed enough times, becomes quieter and also, somehow, more durable.

I drove home in silence.

I thought about his hands.

The valve does not close because we feel too much.

It closes when it is no longer safe to feel — and when, over enough time, no one comes to ask what was lost.

He was not a problem to be managed.

He was a man whose hands remembered the weight of a tomato on the vine, and whose inner life had been slowly erased by a system that had no column for it.

What he needed was not a plan.

What he needed was someone to sit in the room long enough that his own life could come back into focus.

That is where this book begins.

Not with technique. Not with philosophy.

With a man in a chair by a window, and the question he had stopped expecting anyone to ask:

What have you been carrying? And what, underneath the carrying, do you miss?

We will return to him. His story is not finished in this chapter. It is not finished at the end of this book, either — because the people who teach us the most do not stay neatly inside the chapters we assign to them.

But for now, let him sit there. In that chair. In that light.

He is the reason this book exists.

He, and everyone like him — everyone who has been turned into a case file when, all along, they were a person.

You did not close because you were weak. You closed because you were overwhelmed.

There is a place inside every person that learned to close. Not because they were broken. Because they were trying to survive.

The closing was not failure. It was intelligence. The body, encountering something too large or too unsafe to feel in real time, made a decision: not now. We will hold this until it is safe.

The trouble is that the waiting does not end on its own.

Years pass. The original danger is long gone. But the valve stays closed, because no one told it the danger had passed. Because the body — faithful, precise, immune to reasoning — requires not understanding but experience. Not the argument that things are safe. The felt reality of safety, sustained long enough for the nervous system to believe it.

So the pressure builds. It becomes other things: anxiety without a clear cause, anger without a clear target, numbness without a reason. A restlessness that sleep cannot cure and success cannot touch. A distance from your own life you cannot name but cannot quite deny.

We try to fix it. Discipline. Productivity. Positive thinking. Reinvention. We build elaborate strategies for managing the steam without ever addressing the valve.

The valve does not open through force. It opens through safety.

This is not metaphor. This is not philosophy. This is how the body works.

What looks like resistance is protection. What looks like stubbornness is survival. What looks like a person who will not open is a person who has not yet been offered the conditions in which opening feels safe.

That man in the chair by the window was not difficult. He was waiting.

We are all, in some way, waiting.

2

The Body That Learned

Before there was language, there was sensation. Before memory organized experience into story, the body was already responding. Already learning. Already holding.

You were not born with a closed valve.

Watch a young child for five minutes — any child, in any ordinary moment — and you will see something the adult world has largely forgotten: a being fully alive to the present. Crying, laughing, raging, delighted — moving through emotion the way weather moves through an open sky. Nothing lingers. Nothing hardens. The feeling arrives, moves through, and releases.

This is not emotional immaturity. This is the body in its natural state.

Then life happens.

Not catastrophically, necessarily. Often quietly. A raised voice that arrives without warning. A parent who is absent when needed most — not cruelly absent, perhaps not even consciously absent, but absent in the way the body records as: this kind of feeling has no safe receiver here. A silence in a family that communicates, without a single word: certain feelings are not permitted in this house.

The nervous system does not judge these experiences. It simply learns from them. The way water learns the shape of whatever contains it, the body learns the shape of the environment it inhabits.

And slowly, almost imperceptibly, the valve begins to form.

Not in a single moment. Not as a conscious decision. As an accumulation of small adjustments, each one a response to something that actually happened. A held breath here — because breathing fully would have meant crying, and crying was not safe. A smile assembled in the gap between feeling something and showing it. A performance of calm so convincing that, in time, the performer forgets they are performing.

Protection does not begin with thought. It begins with contraction. Layer by layer, the body narrows what it allows through.

If hiding emotion kept the peace, it learned to hide emotion. If being useful kept you loved, it learned to be endlessly useful — even at its own expense. If staying small kept you safe, it learned to stay small. And then went on staying small long after the threat had passed.

By adulthood, the valve feels like personality. Like who you are, not a strategy you developed.

"I'm strong." "I don't need much." "I stay busy."

These are not personality traits. They are adaptive strategies that calcified into identity. And strategies, unlike identities, can be examined. Can be understood. Can be gently, safely, updated.

A child who learned to be quiet may grow into an adult who rarely expresses emotion — not because they feel little, but because feeling became something the body stopped trusting as safe to show. A child who learned that love required performance may grow into an adult who is quietly terrified during any pause in productivity. A child who learned to disappear may become an adult who is very skilled at being absent from the moments that require presence most.

None of these people chose this. The nervous system is not interested in choice. It is interested in survival. It found a strategy. The strategy worked. The strategy became wired.

The cost does not arrive as obvious pain. It arrives as absence.

Joy lands and slides away before it can settle. Success arrives and leaves a strange hollow — as though something essential was not invited to the celebration. Love is present but not fully received: accepted from a slight distance, scanning for the catch, waiting for the condition that will eventually be attached.

Rest feels incomplete. There is a quality of baseline tension that has been present so long it no longer registers as tension. It registers as normal.

And then, slowly, a question forms. Not during crisis. In the pause between meetings. In the quiet after a success that should have felt better than it did.

Why doesn't this feel like enough?

This question is not failure.

It is the valve beginning to speak. The body, after years of silence, asking finally to be heard.

The question itself is the first opening.

PART TWO

A Life That Worked

3

Functioning and Empty

From the outside, everything appeared whole. Inside, a quiet exhaustion held its breath.

Many people who carry a closed valve appear, from the outside, to be exceptionally well. Reliable, capable, often the person others turn to in difficulty. They build careers and families and reputations that look solid from every visible angle.

They would not always identify themselves that way either — because the absence that comes with a closed valve does not feel like pain. It feels like a faint glass wall between you and your own life. A sense that you are watching it more than living it. Present in the room, saying the right things, performing capably — and somewhere behind the performance, something waiting to be let in.

There is a particular exhaustion that comes from performing wholeness for years. Not the tiredness that sleep resolves. The fatigue that accumulates when the body holds, for decades, what it was never meant to hold forever. A weight you stopped noticing because you have been carrying it so long it began to feel like you.

The body communicates this in its own language. Anxiety that rises without explanation. Shoulders that brace and never quite drop. A jaw that tightens through the day. Breath that never quite reaches the belly. Illness that returns, or lingers, or settles precisely in the part of the body where the holding is most concentrated.

These signals are usually treated as problems to eliminate.

But they do not answer what the body is actually asking.

What am I holding back from myself?

I remember the first time that question found me. Not in a moment of crisis. In a corridor, after a meeting that had gone well. By every external measure, things were fine.

I noticed, standing there, that I felt almost nothing.

Not sad. Not numb in any dramatic sense. Simply absent from myself. Present enough to perform the role — and somewhere behind the performance, something waiting. Something that had stopped asking to be included because it had learned not to expect an invitation.

That was the threshold. Not a breakdown. Not a revelation. A moment of honest seeing.

The valve, visible for the first time.

4

The Man Who Called Rest Laziness

He was the kind of man who defined himself by what he could endure. He wore his capacity for work like armor. He had built a business from nothing, raised a family, accumulated the evidence of a life well-constructed.

When illness arrived, he treated it as an obstacle. He applied what had always worked: effort. Discipline. The refusal to stop.

His body was unimpressed. It had been signaling for years — tightening here, aching there, sending fatigue that deepened with each season — and been answered every time with more output. The illness was simply the body's final escalation. The loudest signal in a long sequence that had all been ignored.

What eventually helped him was the opposite of everything he knew how to offer himself. Stopping. Lying in a quiet room. Allowing his wife to bring him things. Saying, for the first time in memory: I am not fine.

Allowing himself to be tired — visibly, without immediately trying to resolve the tiredness into something more manageable.

The illness was not punishment. It was communication. The body finding, at last, a language loud enough to hear.

What changed for him was not a technique. It was a relationship — with his own body. He began, for the first time, to treat its signals as information rather than inconvenience.

He did not become less capable. He became more present. And presence, it turned out, was what his family had been asking for all along.

5

The Body Speaks

The King's voice was never broken. It was guarded. He did not heal through technique. He healed through trust.

There is a scene in the 2010 film The King's Speech that I return to again and again.

Bertie — who will become King George VI — is sitting in a small, ordinary room with Lionel Logue, a speech therapist from Australia who treats him, deliberately and consistently, as an equal. Not with disrespect. With something rarer, in the world Bertie inhabits: ordinariness. Logue calls him by his given name. He makes him sit on the floor. He brings levity when the King's rigidity begins to tighten around the work.

He creates, carefully, an environment without hierarchy — which is to say, without the particular danger that had taught Bertie's body to guard itself.

The stammer was not a mechanical failure. It was a valve. The voice — that most intimate expression of a person, the thing that carries not just words but presence, intention, self — had learned to withhold. It had learned, in a childhood watched by a cold father, in a court requiring constant performance, in a body never permitted to be uncertain in public, that full expression was unsafe.

The voice tightened around what it had been taught was inadmissible.

Logue understood, intuitively if not theoretically, that the body will not open under judgment. It will not open under pressure. It opens under relationship. Under the slow, unconditional experience of being in the presence of someone who will not shame it for what it does.

He gave Bertie something royal protocol had never permitted: equality, humor, and the unspoken assurance that failure in this room would not be held against him.

The valve opened not because of the exercises. It opened because of the safety that surrounded them.

This is the law that governs all opening: the body speaks when it knows it will not be shamed for speaking.

We see this everywhere, once we know to look. The person who can only cry alone. The professional who is articulate in meetings and inarticulate with their own children. The caregiver who gives everything to others and cannot receive a kind word without deflecting it — "Oh, it's nothing," "Don't worry about me" — as though receiving care were a vulnerability they cannot afford.

These are not character flaws. They are maps of where safety has and has not been established.

6

The Nurse Who Had Not Cried in Twenty Years

She was good at her job in the particular way that closed valves make people good at difficult work. Steady. Reliable. She could sit with dying patients and their families, holding space for grief she did not allow herself.

She had learned early that emotional expression on the ward was a liability. Not because anyone said so explicitly. The environment made it clear enough. The nurses who wept were whispered about. The ones who stayed composed were trusted. The lesson was absorbed without being spoken.

So she compressed. Year by year, the valve closing incrementally, each small compression feeling like professionalism. By twenty years in, she had stopped noticing she was doing it.

The compression had become identity.

One afternoon, a colleague said something small. Genuinely meant.

“I see how hard you work. I hope you know it matters.”

She excused herself to the bathroom and stood at the sink, weeping, for a long time, unable to stop.

Nothing had broken. Something had opened.

What she wept for she could not entirely name. Not grief for anything specific. The release of an accumulation — twenty years of moments that had needed exactly this response and been denied it. Twenty years of holding, finally given permission to set itself down.

She told me later she had been frightened. She thought she was having a breakdown.

She was not breaking down. She was breaking open. The valve, receiving the message it had waited two decades to hear:

You do not have to hold everything alone.

INTERLUDE

7

A Bench, A Park, A Quiet Mind

There are afternoons I have spent in a park. Not meditating, not doing anything purposeful. Simply sitting. Watching the light move across the ground. Letting the noise of the day settle the way sediment settles when water stops being agitated.

In that particular quietness — the kind that comes not from trying to be quiet but from simply stopping — things begin to surface. Thoughts I did not know I was carrying. Patterns I could not have articulated in a meeting. A way of watching my own thinking from slightly outside it, as though the quiet creates a small but real distance between the watcher and the watched. In that distance, something becomes visible that was invisible a moment ago: how old some of my habitual fears are. How little they belong to the present moment.

Sometimes I catch myself mid-thought — rehearsing an old anxiety, replaying a fear that has no current cause — and the stillness simply shows it for what it is. Not through analysis. Through perspective.

The park does not explain the thought. It creates enough quiet that the thought can no longer pass unseen.

I believe most people have had moments like this — in a park, in a shower, on a long drive, in the suspension just before sleep — and most have dismissed them. Called them daydreaming. Called them unproductive.

They are not unproductive. They are the valve, communicating through the only channel the conscious mind has left it.

The subconscious does not need you to adopt a formal practice. It needs you to stop overriding it long enough to be heard. It speaks the moment you stop drowning it out.

When I sit still long enough, something is already present. Already knowing. Already waiting to be asked. That something is what this whole book is about.

8

What the Night Knows

The dreaming mind speaks the language the waking mind has forgotten. It does not argue. It shows.

The subconscious is not mysterious. It is simply the part of you that remembers everything.

Every experience. Every emotion. Every moment that felt too large or too unsafe to process in real time. It stores all of it — not as stories, but as sensation. As physical pattern. As the body's automatic way of moving through the world.

We have spent years trusting only what the conscious mind can access and explain. We call the rest irrational. Noise. But the subconscious does not stop its work because it has been dismissed. It continues, faithfully — in sleep, in the body's tension, in the feeling that arrives without explanation, in the knowing that precedes any reason. It speaks in the language it knows: image, sensation, symbol — the compressed poetry of the body's inner life.

I began paying attention to my dreams when the park afternoons first showed me that the waking mind was not the only mind I had.

Something in the stillness had loosened — the quiet had cracked something open. The dreams walked through the crack.

I dreamed once of traveling with others, carrying a small tube of blood. Something about it felt sacred. We approached a gate. A guard saw the blood and rushed toward us, alarmed — treating something vital as though it were dangerous. Before he reached us, something intervened. Later, I found a hidden passage and slipped down into a lower level. Three large men entered — radiating something ancient, unhurried. One of them smiled and said, simply: there is nothing wrong with receiving help sometimes.

I woke and sat with it for a long time. The blood — something vital, carefully carried — treated as dangerous by the very people guarding the gate. The hidden passage. The elders arriving with permission.

You are allowed to receive.

I dreamed of rooftops and exposure — standing in the open with nowhere to hide. My mother arriving with a suit so I could be covered. The suit not quite fitting. And the discovery that I could choose not to go where others were being taken, simply because they were going.

I am vulnerable. And I am still worthy of being here.

I dreamed of a slice of brilliant yellow light entering my body like gentle lightning. No effort. No seeking. Only receiving. I woke flooded with something that felt like love, though no person or situation was attached to it. Simply grace — arriving without condition, without needing to be deserved.

Each dream loosened something. Not through interpretation but through contact — the dreaming body reaching places waking reason could not access.

There is a part of you that has been speaking all along. In dreams, in the body's signals, in the emotion that surfaces for no visible reason, in the thought that appears when the mind is finally still enough to see it.

That part is not broken. It is not irrational. It is the deepest intelligence you carry — patient, persistent, waiting only for enough quiet to be heard.

When you begin to listen, the valve begins to trust that listening is possible. And trust is how it opens.

PART THREE

The Crack of Light

9

What Cannot Be Unseen

Awareness does not arrive with drama. It arrives as a pause. A small gap between the stimulus and the old response. In that gap, everything becomes possible.

Awareness begins as noticing.

Not analysis. Not intention. Not a decision to improve. Simply a moment in which something that was invisible becomes visible. A tiny gap opens between you and your automatic response — and in that gap, for the first time, you can see what has been happening.

I remember the first time I noticed the valve in real time. I was in a conversation that should have been easy — a catch-up with someone I liked, no stakes. Somewhere in the middle of it, a familiar tightening gripped my chest. A slight narrowing, as though a part of me had quietly stepped back from the room without the rest of me noticing it leave.

I had felt this a thousand times. I had never seen it before.

The difference between feeling something and seeing it is the difference between being inside a weather system and watching it from a window. Both are real. But only one offers perspective.

Seeing the tightening did not change it. It was still there. But there was a new quality to being with it: a small distance between the sensation and my identification with it. The tightening was something happening in me. It was not me. And that distinction, though it sounds simple, had enormous consequences.

If the tightening was not me, I could be curious about it. I could ask: Where did you come from? What are you protecting? What is it you remember that I am no longer in?

The asking was enough.

Once you see it, you cannot unsee it. This is not a curse. It is the beginning of a different kind of freedom.

I began to notice patterns as they occurred: the chest tightening before certain conversations — not dangerous conversations, simply ones that required a presence the valve had not learned to trust. The held breath before rest, as though stopping required permission I was still waiting to receive. The automatic pivot toward activity whenever sitting still threatened to let something surface.

None of this was new. What was new was the seeing.

There was, strangely, relief in this. Not because the tightening went away. But because seeing clearly — even painful things, even things you cannot yet change — is its own kind of freedom. You know where you are. You know what you are working with.

What is seen clearly begins to release naturally. You do not have to make yourself open. You have to stop preventing yourself from opening.

That is the entire practice. That is the whole work.

10

What Was Never Yours to Carry

The shame that does not belong to you is the heaviest shame of all — because you have been carrying it under someone else's name.

There is a particular kind of weight that closes the valve faster than almost any other. It is the weight of a shame that is not yours.

A shame that was handed to you. A shame you did not earn. A shame that belonged, originally, to someone else — to their fear, their limitation, their need to feel larger by making you smaller — and that you accepted, because accepting it was easier than refusing it, and because refusing it, in that moment, did not feel safe.

I have watched this happen in hospital corridors. A nurse answers a phone. A surgeon, frightened by something in his own day, turns on her — sharp voice, small humiliation, the kind that leaves no mark except the one it leaves inside. She has done nothing wrong. She was doing her job, correctly, the way she has done it a thousand times before. And yet she apologizes. She lowers her voice. She folds something inside herself that did not need to be folded. The shame that belonged to his fear is now living in her chest, and by the end of the shift it will feel like hers.

I have watched this happen at kitchen tables. A husband is told, across years, that he is too much, too tired, too quiet, too something. He begins to make himself smaller. He speaks less. He takes up less space. He accepts, without knowing he has accepted, that his presence is a burden. The shame that belonged to the other person's overwhelm is now living in him. He will carry it into rooms where it does not apply, with people who never asked it of him.

I have watched this happen in families. A child is told that her feeling is wrong, her question is wrong, her want is wrong. Not once. A thousand times, in small ways, by people who loved her imperfectly. She learns that her interior is the problem. Decades later, as an adult, she still flinches before she speaks, still apologizes for her own existence, still accepts blame that was never hers. The shame that belonged to her parents' limits is living in her, and she has learned to call it by her name.

I have watched this happen in my own life. A comment, from someone who meant no harm or meant every bit of it, pressing on an old place. The old voice rising: maybe they are right. Maybe you are too much. Maybe you are too foreign. Maybe you are too broken. Maybe you should soften. Maybe you should shrink. Maybe you should carry this, too, so they do not have to.

And every time, the same mechanism. A shame that was not mine, asking to be taken in. Asking to close the valve another small degree.

Here is what I want you to know, as clearly as I know how to say it.

The smallness you were asked to become was never the truth about you. It was the truth about the person who needed you smaller.

The surgeon who berated the nurse was afraid. The fear was his. The shame he spilled on her was a shame he could not carry himself.

The partner who made you feel like too much was overwhelmed. The overwhelm was theirs. The diminishment they handed you was a weight they could not hold alone.

The parent who could not meet your feeling was at the end of what they knew. Their limit was theirs. The wrongness you absorbed was never in you. It was in the gap between what you needed and what they were able to give.

The culture that closed its door when you did not follow its rules was protecting itself. Its rigidity was its own. The exile you felt was not a verdict on you. It was a report on how much that culture could not yet bear.

None of it was yours.

You have been carrying it under someone else's name for a very long time.

The first movement of opening the valve, when the weight is a shame that does not belong to you, is not forgiveness and not analysis. It is simpler than that.

It is seeing.

Seeing, clearly, that the weight has a different address than the one it has been living at. That it was delivered to you by mistake, or by cruelty, or by the ordinary incapacity of people doing their best with what they had — and that you signed for it, because you were a child, or because you were tired, or because refusing it in that moment did not feel possible.

You signed for a package that was never yours. You have been carrying it ever since.

You do not have to carry it anymore.

The body will not release what the mind has not yet seen. So the work, first, is to see.

To notice, quietly, when a small voice rises in you and says you should make yourself smaller — and to ask, gently: whose voice is that? Who benefited from me becoming small? Whose shame was I being asked to carry? And is that shame still mine to hold?

Often, when you ask, the answer comes. Not dramatically. Just a small, quiet recognition: this was never mine.

And in that recognition, something begins to loosen. Not because you have forced anything. Because something you were holding has been seen for what it is, and what is seen clearly begins, on its own, to release.

Then — and only then — comes the movement toward love.

Not love for the one who handed you the shame. That may come later, or it may not; it is not required. Love, first, for yourself. For the version of you who accepted the weight because they had to. For the younger body that closed because closing was the only available kindness. For the person you had to become to survive what was not yours to begin with.

That person did not fail. That person carried, faithfully, a burden that should never have been placed in their arms. And they carried it for you, until you were strong enough to set it down.

You are strong enough now.

I will not make myself smaller so that you can feel larger. And I will not ask you to make yourself smaller either. We are here, in whatever size we actually are. The valve opens in bodies that have stopped apologizing for the space they take up.

This is not defiance. This is not anger. This is the quiet, ordinary sanity of a person returning to their own name.

The shame that was not yours is being returned, gently, to its owner. You may never speak of the return. You may never see the person whose weight you carried. That is not the point. The point is that the weight, in your body, has been renamed. It is no longer "my failure," "my wrongness," "my too-muchness." It is, at last, "what I was handed, and what I am now setting down."

And in the setting down, the breath returns. Not all at once. A little more, each time you remember. A little more, each time you notice the small voice rising and answer it, now, with the larger one.

I was never too much. I was never too small. I was never the wrong shape for the room. The room was smaller than my life, and the life was trying, all along, to be lived.

The valve opens when it is finally permitted to hold only what is actually yours. Which is so much less than you have been holding. And so much more worth carrying.

11

The Descent

The descent is not collapse. It is the willingness to be present with your own life without turning away.

Descent does not look like progress.

It looks like standing still while something deeper rearranges itself. Less, not more. Less certainty, less momentum, a slower and more careful relationship with each day. The tools that worked before — control, productivity, the performance of capability — still function, technically. But they no longer satisfy. The engine runs and the destination feels wrong.

After awareness arrives, the mind wants results. It has seen the valve. It wants to fix it. It wants a program, a timetable, measurable progress.

This phase does not offer that.

It offers something quieter and more essential: the capacity to feel what has been held.

Grief arrives. Sometimes without a specific object — a sadness that predates any particular loss. This is often the grief of the younger self who did not receive what they needed. The child who learned to be strong. The teenager who learned to be invisible. The young adult who became so skilled at managing their interior life that they lost access to it.

Anger surfaces. Not hot, not explosive — slow and honest. A reckoning with what was endured, what was accepted that should not have been, what was given away that deserved to be kept. This anger is not destructive. It is the body declaring: this mattered. What happened to me was real.

Tenderness comes for younger versions of the self. Not sentimentally. Genuinely. The recognition that the child who closed the valve was not weak or wrong. They were doing the best that could be done with the resources available.

These are not signs of regression. They are signs of thaw.

The Buddha spoke of two arrows. The first is unavoidable: sickness, loss, disappointment, heartbreak. They arrive whether invited or not. The second arrow is the one we fire ourselves. The replaying of the moment. The blame. The shame. The conviction that we should have been stronger, should have known, should have handled it differently. The resistance to what has already happened, as though force of will can retroactively change the past.

The second arrow hurts far more than the first. And it is optional.

The valve does not close because of the first arrows. It closes under the accumulated weight of second arrows — years of adding judgment to pain, until the pain is so layered with self-condemnation that the only relief is to stop feeling altogether.

Healing begins when we put down the second arrow.

Not by pretending the first one didn't land. Not by performing acceptance while secretly still in resistance. But by meeting what is here — cleanly, honestly, without the additional cruelty of self-attack — and allowing the body to complete the response it began.

Healing does not follow desire. It follows capacity. The body opens only as fast as it feels safe.

12

The Night My Childhood Sat Next to Me

I was taking my wife to a concert I had booked for her birthday. The evening should have been simple. I loved this woman. I had been looking forward to it.

In the car, she corrected me about something small — the route I was taking, or the way I had handled something earlier. The kind of thing that passes without trace in an ordinary moment.

Something in me did not pass it without trace.

My chest tightened. An interior withdrawal, cold and sudden — the valve closing before I had even registered what was happening.

I knew, sitting there, that I was not responding to her. I was responding to a voice I had heard before she existed in my life — a voice from much earlier, with a specific quality, a specific implication: the way I naturally did things was wrong. I needed correcting. The version of me that acted without guidance was not quite acceptable.

The concert hall dissolved somewhere inside me. I was twelve years old, being told — without anyone raising their voice — that my natural way of being in the world required modification.

She was not doing this. She was simply present in the car, being herself, making a small observation. But the nervous system does not distinguish between what is happening and what it remembers happening. It responds to patterns. And this pattern — the correction, the implied inadequacy, the need to adjust — was written deep.

I went quiet for the rest of the evening. She noticed. She said nothing, because she had learned, by then, to give me space when I went somewhere she couldn't reach.

I did not handle that night gracefully. But I saw it. I saw the valve close, and I recognized, with real clarity, what it was closing around.

Not her correction.

The memory of what correction had meant in the earlier life.

The people we love most often trigger the oldest wounds. Not because they are cruel — but because love creates safety. And in safety, what has been held begins to move.

They are not the cause of the pain. They are the mirror in which we finally see it.

That night, looking into that mirror, something began.

13

The Room That Held Its Breath

Before the first incision, there is a pause.

It has a name. The timeout. A moment written into the fabric of modern surgery — every operating room, every case, without exception — in which the entire team stops what it is doing and speaks aloud, together, the essential facts. The patient's name. The procedure. The site. The side. Any allergies. Any concerns.

It sounds simple. It is. That is the point.

The timeout exists because, for a long time, hospitals did not have one — and people died because of it. Wrong patient. Wrong side. Wrong organ. A surgeon prepping for a right knee while the chart, somewhere, said left. Medicine eventually borrowed the practice from aviation, where pilots had long since learned that the most dangerous errors were not the exotic ones. They were the ordinary ones. The ones that slip through a tired mind on an ordinary day.

Atul Gawande wrote a whole book about it. The checklist. The timeout. The simple, unglamorous act of pausing long enough to be present.

In a good room, the timeout is a kind of settling. A collective exhale. Everyone — surgeon, anesthetist, scrub nurse, circulator — stops performing their individual tasks for thirty seconds and arrives, together, in the same moment.

The patient, unconscious on the table, is the reason.

— — —

I had been assigned to the room that morning. A craniotomy. A surgeon I had never worked with before.

The setup took a long time, the way it always does for a neurosurgical case. The drips prepared and double-checked. The backup drugs laid out in the order I would need them if something went wrong. The pharmacy calls, the labs reviewed, the patient seen, the consent confirmed. My own quiet ritual of preparation — the one I had done thousands of times, the one that had become not performance but presence.

This is the work. Before the work.

I do not rush it. In anesthesia you learn, quickly, that almost every case is uneventful — and that the uneventful cases are the reason you can be trusted with the eventful ones. What keeps a patient alive when something goes wrong is not heroism. It is what was prepared when nothing was wrong.

By the time the surgeon came in, the room was ready. My drugs drawn. My lines secured. My monitors calibrated. The patient asleep, stable, protected.

And then the timeout began.

— — —

Someone across the room answered a phone.

It was the hospital line. A family member, I learned later, with a question. She said a few words — quietly, as people do when they are trying not to disturb — and began to set the phone down.

And the room ruptured.

Not the patient. The patient was unconscious, perfectly held.

The surgeon.

He erupted.

Loud. Disproportionate. The kind of eruption that has a wind-up inside it — a pressure that had not originated in this moment, that had been waiting somewhere for a small enough provocation to justify its release. The phone was not the reason. The phone was the permission.

I felt it in my body before I understood it with my mind.

My shoulders rose. My breath shortened. I watched the nurse's face across the room change — the particular change a face makes when someone who had been doing her job correctly is suddenly being made small for it. Her hand, still holding the phone, went still. She did not defend herself. She did not explain. She absorbed.

She had been trained, somewhere long before this morning, to absorb.

The room did not breathe.

— — —

Here is what I want you to feel, before I explain anything:

A room full of people is a room full of nervous systems. And nervous systems speak to each other whether anyone names it or not. One closed valve, wound tightly enough, can close every valve in the room. The tightening is not metaphorical. It is physiological. Shoulders rise. Breath shortens. The attention that was available for the work narrows into the attention required for survival.

And the patient — unconscious, entirely dependent on the presence of the people above him — does not know any of this. But his body, in some way we are only beginning to understand, is being operated on by a room that is no longer fully in the room.

This is not a small thing. This is the thing.

— — —

We regrouped. We restarted the timeout. We completed it. The procedure began.

But the rupture did not leave. It lived in him, all morning, surfacing in mutters, in sharp asides, in a running commentary that returned again and again to the nurse who had answered the phone. Hours later, she tried once — gently, the way a person tries when they have been absorbing for hours and cannot absorb any more — to explain.

"The family called. I answered because it was the hospital phone. I wasn't doing something."

She did not raise her voice. She did not argue. She simply asked to be seen.

He dismissed her. Loudly.

And I understood, standing at the head of the table — hands free, eyes scanning the monitors the way you learn to scan them, clockwise, twelve o'clock down and around, the whole field taken in as one breath — that something was very wrong. And that what was wrong was not happening in this operating room at all. It was happening somewhere earlier. Somewhere he had been, and could not leave.

— — —

I learned, later, what I had already felt.

This surgeon had a history. Previous cases that had gone wrong in the way cases are not supposed to go wrong. Committees. Reviews. The sustained, private terror of a man who had, more than once, been the reason for the kind of event that the timeout exists to prevent.

He was not raging at a nurse. He was raging at the memory of himself. At what he had done, and could not undo, and could not feel directly, and could not speak about.

So it lived in him. Wound tightly. Ready.

And every small provocation — a phone ringing, a glance misread, a moment of ordinary human imperfection in the room — became a legitimate target for what could not be aimed where it actually belonged.

This is what a closed valve does when it belongs to a person whose work holds the lives of others.

The rest of us simply lived with it. For years, probably. Room after room. Case after case. Because there was no language, in that culture, for what we were all feeling. There was only the case. The procedure. The professional composure that made it possible to continue.

— — —

There were three valves in that room.

His — wound so tight he could no longer tell the present from the past. A man operating on a brain while somewhere inside him a different brain, his own, was still being operated on by everything he had not been able to release.

Hers — the nurse's. The one that had learned, over years, to go small in the presence of larger valves. To absorb. To apologize for her own existence. Not because she was weak. Because she had been trained by environments like this one that absorption was the price of staying in the room.

And mine.

I felt the closing happen in me. I felt the rage rise — not at her, at him. I felt the temptation to tighten. To match his closing with my own. To become, for the rest of the case, the kind of anesthetist who does the work with a jaw set hard against the man across the drape.

And I noticed it.

That was the whole difference. Not that I was above the closing. That I saw the closing as it began.

In the seeing, a small gap opened. And in that gap, a choice became available that would not have been available otherwise: I did not have to add my closing to his.

I could stay with the patient. I could keep scanning — twelve, three, six, nine, and back — the way I had been taught to watch a room without gripping it. I could let the attention settle on the monitors with the particular quality that is not possible when a nervous system is bracing. I could let the nurse feel, without saying anything, that at least one person in the room had not joined the verdict against her.

I did not fix him. I did not rescue her. I did not confront anything.

I simply did not close.

— — —

There is something else I need you to understand about that room. Something that a reader outside medicine may not see on their own.

The closed valve in that surgeon was not only a human problem. It was a safety problem.

Because anesthesia, in a long case, is not a silent job. It runs on a continuous, unhurried conversation across the drape. The patient's rhythm shifts to something new, and I say so. The blood pressure begins to drift down, and I ask what the field looks like — how much has she lost, are we where we thought we would be. I tell the surgeon what I have. Hemoglobin is this. We have two units available. I am sending another gas now. I will let you know what comes back. They tell me what they are seeing. I adjust. They adjust. The labs come. We keep going. The case ends. Everyone goes home.

That is not drama. That is the work.

That quiet two-way current of information is what actually keeps a patient safe through a long operation. Not the heroic moment. The ordinary moments. The hundred small exchanges that nobody would ever think to write down, because none of them, alone, seemed like much.

A closed valve at the head of the drape interrupts that current.

Not dramatically. That is what most people do not understand. It does not stop the room. It does not end the case. It simply makes every small communication cost something that, a moment ago, it did not cost.

The anesthetist thinks twice before saying *pressure is drifting.* The resident thinks three times before asking *is that more bleeding than you expected.* The scrub nurse stops volunteering the small observation she would have volunteered in a calmer room. No one is being insubordinate. No one is being unprofessional. They are simply, unconsciously, calculating the cost of speech in a room where speech has just been punished.

And that calculation — that half-second hesitation, that softened phrasing, that swallowed observation — is the margin by which a patient in a long case gets hurt.

Not in the exotic event. In the ordinary one. The one where someone in the room saw it a little before anyone else did, and did not say it cleanly enough, quickly enough, because the room had just taught them that speaking clearly has a price.

I speak. I have always spoken. I speak in the rooms where the surgeon is kind, and I speak in the rooms where the surgeon is not, because the patient on the table is not interested in the vibe between the people above them. The patient needs the information to move, cleanly and quickly, between the two people who can keep them alive. That is what the job is.

But I have watched, over the years, what a closed valve does to other people's speech. And I have come to believe that a surgeon who cannot regulate his own nervous system is, quietly, a safety event in progress — not because he will do something dramatic, but because he has just made it slightly harder for everyone else in the room to do their ordinary jobs.

This is what the checklist exists to protect. This is what the timeout exists to protect. Not only the catastrophic error. The small, continuous current of ordinary communication that keeps a human being alive on a table for six hours.

All of it — every protocol, every checklist, every timeout — can be quietly undone by one wound-up nervous system at the head of the drape.

The valve is not a private matter when you are the person holding another person's life.

This is one of the reasons I am writing this book.

— — —

This is what I want you to understand about awareness in the places where it matters most.

Awareness does not always look like a dramatic intervention. Very often, it looks like the absence of one. It looks like a nervous system that, in a room full of tightening, quietly does not tighten. A presence that does not amplify what is already in the air.

The nurse, I think, felt it. I do not know. We never spoke about it. In that culture, you do not speak about it. But something in the way she looked at me, once, near the end of the case — a small, almost imperceptible softening — made me believe she had found, in the room, one place where her valve did not have to close all the way.

That is not nothing. In a room like that, on a day like that, it may be the most a person can offer.

— — —

I think about that surgeon sometimes.

I do not think of him with contempt. I think of him the way you eventually come to think of anyone whose closing you have witnessed up close — with a kind of sorrow that does not excuse the harm, but also does not pretend the harm came from nowhere.

He was carrying something enormous. A weight a human being is not built to carry alone. And no one had ever sat down with him long enough — no colleague, no committee, no institution — to help him feel what he had not been able to feel. So it lived in him. And it leaked out, day after day, onto the people around him. Onto the nurses who had answered phones. Onto the residents who had asked questions at the wrong moment. Onto, I have to assume, the people at home.

A closed valve does not stay inside the person who closed.

It spreads. Through rooms. Through families. Through institutions. It shapes what is possible in every space it enters.

And the opposite is also true.

An open valve — or even, on a hard day, a valve that simply does not close further — changes what is possible in the same rooms. Not because it announces itself. Because the nervous systems around it feel the absence of one more closing, and respond, quietly, by not closing quite as hard themselves.

You are not only healing for yourself. You are healing for every room you enter.

— — —

It would be easy, after a story like this, to think the valve is the answer. That if a person could only find their valve, open it, and keep it open, the closings would stop.

That is not quite right.

The valve is not the solution. The valve is *the doorway.*

It is the place in the body where what has been held becomes available to be felt. Without it, the experience remains abstract — an idea about ourselves, a story we tell, a diagnosis we accept. Something we can think about but cannot quite reach.

But the valve alone is not enough.

A person can find their valve and still live there. Wound around it. Managing it. Monitoring it. Turning it into one more thing to get right. The valve, without awareness, becomes another room to get stuck in.

What opened the gap in that operating room was not the valve. It was something quieter. The noticing. The small, unarmored seeing of what was beginning to happen inside me before it completed itself.

That noticing has a name.

Awareness.

The valve gives the body somewhere to feel what is moving through it. Awareness is what allows it to move through, rather than lodge.

One without the other does not work. The valve without awareness becomes a container for what cannot be released. Awareness without the valve remains in the head — clear, perhaps even eloquent, but unable to reach the places in the body where the holding actually lives.

Together, they make something else possible entirely.

A human being who can remain present in a room where others cannot.

Not because they are stronger. Not because they are above what is happening. But because, in the moment the closing begins, a doorway opens inside them — and they see it open, and they do not walk through it.

Everything that follows is an invitation to practice it.

PART FOUR

The Opening

14

What the Body Carries

Emotion is not an event that happens in the head and disappears. It is biology. The body holds what the mind could not survive. And it holds it faithfully, until you are finally ready to feel it.

The body is not a passive vessel for the mind's experience. It is a living record.

Researchers who have studied emotion at the cellular level have shown what contemplative traditions always knew: a feeling is not a mental event that happens to the body. It is a biological event the body participates in entirely. When a feeling is suppressed, it does not vanish. It becomes stored — held, chemically and physically, until conditions are safe enough to allow release.

The body is not malfunctioning when it holds. It is being faithful. It is waiting, with remarkable patience, for you to be ready.

There is another way to see it. Trauma, in the work of those who study the nervous system closely, is not the memory of what happened. It is the energy of what the body was preparing to do — fight, flee, freeze — that was prevented from completing. The body stores this incomplete response not as memory, but as tension, as pattern, as the automatic readiness to defend that fires before a conscious thought forms.

The body wants to finish what it started. Healing is not reliving the past. It is allowing the nervous system to complete the response that circumstances once made impossible.

We see this stored experience everywhere, once we know to look — in the muscle tension that never quite releases, in the nightmares that replay sensation rather than story, in the automatic flinch that arrives before the mind has registered a threat. The body holds the record of what happened not as punishment, but as faithfulness. It waits until someone finally comes to hear it.

The valve metaphor adds the mechanism: the body opens only when it finally believes it is safe to do so. Healing is not adding something new. It is removing the obstruction — the long-held conviction that opening is dangerous — and allowing the body to do what it has always wanted to do.

You can read every book about healing and change nothing. You can understand the mechanisms, cite the research, explain the neuroscience to others with fluency. None of it will open the valve.

What opens the valve is experience. The lived feeling of safety, sustained long enough for the body to believe it.

I have watched this confirmed many times. A person who has been in years of introspective work — articulate about their patterns, capable of explaining their own psychology with precision — and still not changed at the level that matters. Not because the work failed. Because the mind understood while the body remained unconvinced.

And then: a single moment of genuine, unguarded connection. Something that had been closed for decades begins to move.

The method matters less than the message it carries. The nervous system evaluates one thing:

Is it finally safe to open?

When the answer becomes yes — not in the mind, but in the body, felt in the chest and the belly and the throat — the opening begins. Not on a schedule. Not through effort. Through the body finally trusting what the mind has been trying to tell it for years.

15

The Intelligence That Knows

You have been trying to fix yourself for so long. What if there is nothing to fix? What if there is only something to see?

There is a kind of intelligence in you that does not think. It does not plan, strategize, or weigh options.

It simply knows.

It knows when something is wrong in a relationship — before the argument, before any evidence a rational person would accept. It knows when a room is not safe — before anyone raises their voice. It knows when you are lying to yourself — even when you have convinced everyone else.

This intelligence is prior to thought. It exists beneath the accumulated strategies, identities, and learned responses. It is what remains when you stop managing long enough to simply be present.

And it is not separate from love. It is love — but not the kind we were taught to expect. Not the love that performs, accommodates, or needs something returned. The love that sees clearly, without fear, without the distortion of past hurt — and acts from that seeing.

It was never absent. Even in the most defended years — even when the valve was tightest, the performance most complete — something in you knew what was real and what was performance. What was nourishing and what was slowly hollowing you out.

You were simply too busy surviving to hear it.

When the valve is closed, we do not see. We manage. We interpret everything through the filter of what we survived: old threat, old pain, old story. The person across from us is not perceived as themselves. They are perceived as the pattern they fit.

This is why the same arguments repeat in relationships. Why the same fears return regardless of circumstance. Why insight alone does not change the response — because the response is not being generated by the part of us that insights reach.

But when the valve opens — even slightly — something shifts. The present becomes present. The person across the table becomes themselves, not a symbol. The problem before you becomes what it actually is, not the worst version of what it could be.

Action taken from that seeing is not effortful. It simply arises: clean, direct, right. Not because you forced it. Because nothing is in the way.

The valve opens when inner conflict ends. Not when you win the argument against yourself — when you stop having it.

Every argument you wage with your own nature — I should be different, I should feel differently, I should not be this way — closes the valve a little more. Not because self-examination is wrong. Because war with the self consumes the very energy that opening requires. The conflict is itself the tightening.

This is not passivity. It is something more radical: the willingness to be exactly where you are, seeing exactly what is here, without the additional noise of wishing it were otherwise.

From that willingness, real change arises. Not the change you planned. The change the situation actually requires.

You have already felt this intelligence.

Perhaps in a single conversation where nothing was managed, nothing performed — where you said something true and the other person simply received it. You were not thinking about what to say next. You were simply there.

Perhaps in nature, where the thinking mind briefly went quiet and something else looked out through your eyes. Not mystical. Simply presence, unobstructed.

Perhaps in grief — the strange clarity that sometimes arrives the moment you stop resisting what is true. The fighting ends. And in that moment, something that felt unbearable becomes, strangely, bearable.

In all of these moments, you were not trying. You were not fixing or improving or becoming. You were simply here.

You are not on your way to becoming someone who is whole.

You are already whole.

The valve simply learns, slowly, that it is safe enough to show it.

16

Release

They told me my mind was mine. My anger, mine. My fear, mine. My shame, mine. So I carried them like secrets, like sins I was not allowed to speak. But one day I heard a whisper, like wind through an old pipe: "Your mind is not yours alone. It is the mind of humanity." And suddenly, I saw it. The thoughts that had haunted me — the ache, the control, the silent rage — they were not born in me. They were passed down.

The valve does not carry only what happened to you.

It carries what happened to your parents, and their parents, and the long human line extending behind them — all the unexpressed grief, the love that found no form, the rage swallowed because it had nowhere safe to go. The science of epigenetics confirms what wisdom traditions have always known: we inherit not just bodies but patterns. The fears, adaptations, and unresolved survivals of our ancestors leave chemical marks on our genes — marks that shape how we respond to stress and connection and threat before we have had a single experience of our own.

When something surfaces in you that seems too large to belong to your own life — a grief with no specific origin, a fear with no clear object, a shame that predates anything you can consciously remember — consider: you may be feeling something that has been waiting for generations to be felt. You may be, in this moment, the one with enough safety to complete what could not be completed before.

The valve opening in you may be finishing something that began before you were born.

This is not burden. It is context. It shifts the weight of what you carry from "there is something wrong with me" to "there is something ancient in me, asking to be completed."

The release does not always look like peace.

Sometimes it looks like trembling. Like sighing that arrives without cause. Like warmth moving through the body, then cold — as something long frozen begins to thaw. Like tears that are not sad, exactly, but necessary: the body completing a transaction long deferred. Like breath that drops, without effort, lower in the chest.

These are not signs of breakdown. They are signs of integration.

Many people have a profound opening — in a ceremony, in meaningful work with a professional, in a moment of love that reaches somewhere long defended — and return to ordinary life expecting to remain changed. They find, after a few days or weeks, that the old patterns have reasserted themselves.

This is not failure. It is the body testing safety. Checking: does the world still allow this? Is it truly safe to be open in my actual life?

The answer is built slowly, through repetition. Through small honest moments, sustained over time. Through the practice of staying with discomfort long enough to feel it move — rather than managing it back into storage.

True integration changes the pace itself. Not just how you feel, but how you live.

17

When Trauma Becomes Wisdom

There is a turning point that is difficult to describe until you have passed it. It is the moment when what you carried stops feeling like damage and begins to feel like depth.

Not because the pain was good. Not because you are grateful for what hurt you — that is a performance of acceptance, not the real thing. But because you have stayed with it long enough, seen it clearly enough, that it has ceased to be the enemy and has become, instead, part of the territory you know.

The wound hurts. The wound frightens. And then, with enough time and enough honest presence, a different understanding arrives: the wound became the teacher. The closed valve became the thing that pointed you, eventually, toward the opening. The very defenses that kept you from living fully were also, in some way, what kept you alive long enough to find your way through.

This does not mean the wound was good. It means the wound can be metabolised.

On the other side of the valve opening, there is a kind of compassion that does not require effort. Not just for yourself, but for others. For the parents who were themselves carrying closed valves. For the whole long human inheritance of suffering — passed down, compressed, held, waiting for someone with enough safety to finally feel it.

That compassion is not weakness. It is the clarity of someone who has stopped fighting the past and begun, at last, to inhabit the present.

The wound became a vaccine. The thing that was survived became the thing that made the survival of others possible.

PART FIVE

LIVING OPEN

18

The World Begins to Appear

There is something no one told me to expect.

Not peace, exactly. Not the absence of difficulty. Something quieter than that, and stranger:

The world begins to appear.

I remember the first time I noticed it — not in meditation, not in a moment I had prepared for. I was in a conversation that had started to turn. Someone I care about, frustrated, saying something sharp. The familiar tightening arrived. I felt it come.

And then something different happened.

I watched it come.

There was a small gap — a breath's worth of distance — between the tightening and me. And in that gap, something became visible that had never been visible before:

I know this feeling. I know exactly where it lives. This is the valve, closing around something old.

Not her frustration. Something much earlier than her frustration.

I did not handle it perfectly. But I did not disappear into it either. And that distance — that single breath of seeing — was everything.

— — —

This is what the other side of the work feels like. Not invulnerability. Not the end of being triggered.

The trigger arrives. You feel it arrive. And somewhere in the feeling, a quiet recognition surfaces:

Oh. I see you.

Not with judgment. Not with the second arrow of why am I still like this. Simply with the clarity of someone who has learned to read the weather from a window rather than being inside the storm without knowing it.

The argument that used to swallow you whole — you begin to see it differently. Not the content of the argument. The mechanics of it. Two nervous systems, both closing. Two valves, both trying to protect something old. Two people, neither of them fully in the present moment, both of them somewhere earlier, somewhere smaller, fighting a battle that was never really about this.

And when you can see that — when you can feel the valve closing and know it for what it is — something extraordinary becomes possible.

You can choose not to go to war with it.

— — —

And then the world that was always there begins to come through.

The tree you have walked past a hundred times. The particular quality of afternoon light on a wall. The bird doing exactly what birds do, completely indifferent to everything you are carrying, alive in a way that asks nothing of you.

These things were always there.

The closed valve does not make them disappear. It simply makes them invisible — filtered out by the background noise of a nervous system always scanning, always bracing, always preparing for the next thing that will require managing.

When the valve opens, even slightly, the scanning quiets. And in the quiet, the world steps forward.

Not dramatically. The way a sound becomes audible when the room stops being noisy. The way a face becomes visible when you stop looking past it.

You begin to notice that you are here. That this moment — ordinary, unremarkable, not yet arrived at its meaning — is actually the moment. Not preparation for something else. Not a corridor between significant events.

The thing itself.

— — —

An open valve sees before it names. It meets what is here before deciding what it means.

This is not a philosophy. It is a felt experience — and once you have felt it, even briefly, you cannot unfeel it. You know the difference between looking and seeing. Between hearing and listening. Between being present in a room and actually inhabiting it.

— — —

The stew does not disappear. Life still has its arguments, its frustrations, its ordinary friction. People you love will still say things that land wrong. Circumstances will still arrive that ask more than you feel ready to give.

But you begin to develop a relationship with the stew.

You can be in it and watch it. You can feel the heat and know:

This is not the whole truth of what is happening.

You can be triggered and, in the same moment, recognize the trigger for what it is — not a verdict on the present, but an echo from somewhere earlier, asking finally to be heard.

And in that recognition, something lightens.

Not because the difficulty goes away.

Because you are no longer entirely inside it.

— — —

This is what the open valve offers the world around you, too.

The person across from you — caught in their own stew, their own closing, their own ancient and unfinished business — feels something different in your presence. Not because you have said the right thing. Because you are not adding your closing to their closing.

You become, without trying, a small clearing.

A place where the nervous system of another person can, for a moment, stop bracing.

You do not have to announce this. You do not have to intend it. It simply happens — the way light happens, the way warmth happens, the way a door left open changes the quality of the air in a room without anyone having to explain it.

The valve opens.

And the world, which was always beautiful, begins to be seen.

19

After the Opening

After initiation, life does not reset. The same relationships, responsibilities, and routines remain. What changes is not the world. What changes is how the body meets it.

An open valve does not remove difficulty.

Traffic still exists. Conflict still happens. People you love disappoint you, and you disappoint them. Loss arrives, as it always arrives, because love and loss are not separate things.

What changes is not the weather.

What changes is your relationship to the weather.

A body that is no longer tightened against life has more of itself available for life. Not more time — the hours remain what they are. More presence. More of you, actually inhabiting what is happening rather than processing it from behind a partition.

Conversations deepen — not because you have become more eloquent, but because you are listening differently. When the body is not simultaneously managing its own anxiety while appearing to attend to another person, something else becomes possible: you actually hear what is being said. Not the interpretation. Not the implication you were prepared to find. What is actually there.

Relationships shift. The nervous system stops running its habitual threat assessments on the people closest to you — the background scanning for when the love becomes conditional, when the catch reveals itself. Something relaxes in the air between you. Something that required constant maintenance quietly stops requiring it.

You become easier to love. Not because you are more pleasing. Because there is less performance between you and the people trying to reach you.

Old triggers return. They always do. The body does not erase its history. What changes is your relationship to the trigger when it arrives.

Before: the trigger arrives, the valve closes, the old pattern runs, and somewhere after the fact you reconstruct what happened and wonder why you responded that way again.

After: the trigger arrives. You feel it arrive. There is a pause — brief, real — in which something is visible. I know this feeling. I know where it comes from. I know it is not the whole truth of what is happening right now.

In that pause, choice becomes possible. Not always exercised. Not perfectly. But available.

And then more available. And then more.

The nervous system learns safety through repetition, not through intention. Each moment of choosing differently rewrites the pattern, slowly.

20

The Inner Jail and the Clean No

There is a kind of inner prison no court orders. It is built from the accumulated times we said yes when we meant no, agreed when we disagreed, accepted what we knew was wrong because challenging it felt too costly.

The cost does not stay in the moment. It accumulates. It settles in the chest as a weight. It curls the posture. It erodes the inner sense that you know what is true and can act from it.

The body knows when a line has been crossed. The stomach tightens. The breath shallows. Something goes quiet and watchful — the way an animal goes still when it senses a threat it cannot yet name.

The clean no — the one that arises from the intelligence that knows, without anger, without drama, without needing to justify itself at length — is one of the clearest signs that the valve has opened. It requires no performance. It is simply true. And the body, in the moment of saying it, does not tighten.

It settles.

The greatest freedom is not walking out of a prison. It is walking out of the one you built inside yourself.

21

Living Without a Script

As the valve opens, identity becomes more fluid. Not unstable — fluid. Responsive rather than rehearsed. Capable of being genuinely surprised. Capable of changing its mind without the change feeling like a catastrophic loss of self.

Conversations change when the body is allowed to participate fully. Things are said that were not planned. The right word arrives not from a catalog of appropriate responses but from somewhere present and immediate. The conversation becomes an actual meeting of two people, rather than a managed exchange between two performances.

Defensiveness softens. Not because you become someone without edges — because you learn the difference between a boundary and a wall. A boundary says: I know where I end and where you begin, and I can hold that clearly. A wall says: I do not trust this situation enough to be genuinely present in it.

An open valve knows the difference.

In work, in parenting, in leadership: you become able to hold others without needing to control them. Containment is not control. Containment says: I am steady enough here that you are safe to be unsteady. I will not flinch at your difficult feelings. My stability is not contingent on your being fine.

This is what others feel in the presence of someone whose valve is open. Not authority. Not performance. Presence.

22

It Is Okay to Receive Help

Many people who find this book have been trying to heal alone for years. Carrying the project of their own wellbeing as a private weight, believing that needing help is weakness — or evidence that they have not yet worked hard enough.

Help is not a step backward. Help is a doorway.

The nervous system does not open because we demand it. It opens when it finally believes it is safe. And sometimes building that safety requires external structure: scaffolding that allows deeper change to occur without the risk of collapse.

Working with a skilled professional, when it is the right fit, creates a relationship in which the nervous system can practice being open. Not through technique alone, but through the repeated experience of being received without judgment. The body learns: it is safe to be uncertain here. Safe to not know. Safe to feel without the feeling being immediately managed.

Medication, when genuinely needed, is not failure. It creates neurochemical conditions in which the nervous system has enough stability to begin the work it has been deferring. To use medication while telling yourself you should not need it is to fire the second arrow while the first is still in flight.

Community — the experience of being genuinely known by more than one person — teaches the nervous system something solitary work cannot: that safety is possible not just in one carefully chosen relationship, but as a general condition of life.

The nervous system does not care about the method. It cares about the message: you are no longer alone in this.

That message — however imperfectly it arrives — is often enough to begin.

23

The Gold in the Charcoal

On what rises, and what it really is.

When the valve begins to open, things rise. Grief rises. Rage rises. Old tightness, old weight, sometimes what feels like a dark charcoal energy sitting in the chest or the belly. The first instinct is almost always the same: push it out. Breathe it away. Get rid of it.

But that is force. And force does not work here. What rose did not rise to be evicted. It rose because, for the first time, it felt safe enough to surface. If you push it out, you are telling it once again that it is not welcome — and it will go back down, wait, and compress itself tighter than before.

Then there is the second trap, which is quieter and harder to see. Once you learn not to push, the mind hears the teaching and turns it into a job. *Let me open. Let me open.* Now opening is the project. The ego has simply changed its clothes. It has stopped forcing outwardly and begun forcing inwardly, which is the same forcing with better manners. This is what Krishnamurti kept pointing at when he spoke of the effort to be free as itself a form of bondage. The one who is trying to open is the one in the way.

You do not have to make yourself open.

You only have to notice that you were closing,

and quietly stop.

And then, something most teachings do not say clearly enough: what rises is not waste.

The charcoal is not darkness. The charcoal is compressed energy. It is life force that had nowhere safe to move, so it took the shape of whatever it had to become in order to survive. Grief is love that had nowhere to go. Rage is strength that was never allowed to protect. Fear is intelligence that was trying, all along, to keep you alive. None of it is garbage. None of it is the enemy.

Carl Jung pointed at this a hundred years ago when he spoke of the gold hidden in the shadow. He taught that the work is not to eliminate what has been disowned but to integrate it, because everything you have pushed away still carries the energy you most need. The person who has faced their rage has access to strength. The person who has faced their grief has access to love. The charcoal is the gold, seen from the other side of the pressure.

Ram Dass taught the same truth more tenderly. What you have been running from, he suggested, is the same thing that will set you free. He did not ask people to get rid of their neuroses. He asked them to love their neuroses — to meet them so gently and so often that the neuroses relaxed and revealed what they had been protecting all along. His teacher Maharaj-ji laughed at the idea of meditating anger away. Love everyone, he said — including the angry one.

Krishnamurti went further still. The division itself — *this is bad energy, this is good energy* — is the trap. Energy is just energy. The labeling is what keeps it stuck. When you stop calling it charcoal and stop calling it gold and simply let it be what it is, it moves on its own toward its right use.

David Hawkins mapped the same truth clinically. Low-frequency states — shame, guilt, fear, anger — are not bad. They are dense. Compressed. And when they are fully felt and allowed to release, the energy does not disappear. It rises. Anger becomes courage. Grief becomes acceptance, and then love. Nothing is discarded. Everything is transmuted.

The tantric traditions said it most boldly of all: poison becomes medicine when you know how to hold it. The same force that destroys you when you resist it heals you the moment you stop. Same energy. Different relationship.

Charcoal and gold are the same carbon.

The only difference is pressure, and time,

and whether it was ever allowed to breathe.

So when something rises, do not rush to release it. Do not rush to keep it either. Let it be there. Let it be seen. What is seen clearly begins to release on its own — and what releases does not vanish. It returns to you as the energy it always was, before the world taught it to hide.

This is why the people who have truly surrendered are not empty. They are more alive, not less. More present, not less. More powerful, not less. The work was never to lose anything. The work was to stop compressing what was always yours.

That is the whole teaching.

Nothing to discard. Everything to reclaim.

24

Returning

These are not techniques for fixing the self. They are invitations to relate differently to the places that have been holding for years. Nothing is forced. Everything is welcomed.

What follows is not a program — there is no schedule to complete, no stage to reach, no moment at which the work is declared done.

These are practices for ordinary days — ways of listening to the body that, done with some consistency, teach the nervous system something it may never have been taught:

It is safe to feel. It is safe to surface. It is safe to release.

25

For Noticing

Pause. Once, in an ordinary moment — not in crisis. In the ordinary ones, where the valve's habits are easiest to see.

Feel where your body is holding. Not to fix it. Simply to notice that it is there. Where does something brace? Where is the breath shallow? Where does something feel compressed?

Ask, without demand: What are you protecting right now?

Wait. The body speaks in sensation before it speaks in words. Allow it to be information rather than something to be resolved.

26

For Allowing

Practice saying, once today: I do not need to force anything open.

Rest without earning it. Not as reward, not as recovery from effort — simply as something the body is permitted to have. Sit without an agenda. Walk slowly. Let the exhale be longer than the inhale.

If it helps: let the valve write to you — the nervous system speaking in its own voice, the part of you that has been standing guard. What has it been holding? What has it been protecting you from? What does it need you to understand before it can stand down?

27

For Returning

When the old pace reasserts itself — and it will — do not punish yourself for the return. Simply notice.

Naming what is happening — quietly, without drama, without self-criticism — is itself an act of seeing. And what is seen clearly begins to release naturally.

I see you. I am not running from you.

That acknowledgment alone tells the body something it has been waiting to hear: it is safe to surface. What has been held does not have to be held in secret.

28

For Daily Life

Gentleness. Not as performance — as a genuine orientation toward your own experience. What would you say to a friend who felt exactly this way right now?

Sleep. Nutrition. The reduction of unnecessary chaos. These are not secondary to the emotional work. They are the conditions in which the emotional work becomes possible. An exhausted nervous system cannot process what it holds. It can only manage.

Small truths, shared carefully. One honest thing, to one honest person, in a moment when honesty feels risky but not catastrophic. The body learns that honesty does not destroy. And each time this is confirmed, the valve loosens a little more.

There is no such thing as falling behind in this work. There is only returning. And returning is the practice.

29

A Quiet Hour at the End of the Day

I want to tell you about a moment that had no drama in it at all.

It was late. A long day was closing. I was walking out to my car when I noticed a man sitting on a low bench at the edge of the lot. He was not in distress — not visibly. He was simply sitting, hands loose in his lap, looking at nothing in particular.

I had seen him before, in passing, over the months. I knew only a little: he was carrying something long and difficult at home. A family member who was struggling in ways that had become the organizing fact of his life. He was the kind of person who would answer "how are you" with "getting through it" and mean that as a complete and honest answer.

I sat down beside him on the bench.

He didn't say anything for a moment. Neither did I.

Then he said: "I keep thinking there's something I should be doing. Something I've missed. Some right thing."

He wasn't asking me. He was saying it the way people say things they've been carrying alone for so long that eventually the weight just speaks for itself.

He was quiet again. A long quiet.

Then something happened that I have thought about many times since. His shoulders dropped. Not dramatically — barely visibly. The way a breath releases at the end of a long day when you finally sit down and there is nowhere left to go. The way the body lets go of something it has been bracing against when it finally believes, in some small way, that the bracing is no longer required.

He didn't say anything. He didn't need to.

We sat there for a few more minutes. The lot was still.

Eventually he stood up, nodded once — the kind of nod that means thank you without making anything of it — and walked to his car.

I don't know what shifted for him that night. I don't think it was anything I said. I think it was the sitting. The not needing him to be anywhere other than where he was. The absence of one more person waiting for him to have the answer.

His nervous system had been braced for a very long time. Holding the weight of someone he loved as though the holding itself were a form of protection.

For a few minutes on a bench, it was allowed to put itself down.

That is all the valve ever asks for. A moment in which the bracing is not required. A presence that does not need you to be further along than you are.

It does not take much. But it has to be real.

30

What He Gave Back

You do not choose, in the moment, to keep an open valve. You act from it, and only understand afterward what moved through you.

I want to return to the man I introduced at the beginning of this book.

The man in the chair by the window. The one who told me, near the end of our first hour together, that he had not touched dirt in six years.

I went back the next week. And the week after that.

I did not have a plan. I simply had the memory of his hands resting in his lap, and the quiet understanding that something in me had answered something in him, and that the answer was not yet finished.

He was guarded, at first. Not hostile. Careful. A man who had been visited by many professionals in his life, and had learned that the visits usually ended the same way — with him being moved, or medicated, or reclassified, or left.

He watched me for weeks before he began to trust that this was not the prelude to another departure.

And then, slowly, he began to open.

He told me about his wife. He told me what she had made for dinner on Sundays. He told me the names of his children and the last time he had seen each one. He told me that he had been a man who fixed things — engines, fences, broken radios, the small domestic emergencies of a life lived close to the ground — and that it had been a long time since he had been allowed to be useful.

That word stayed with me. *Allowed.*

A human being is not meant to be a sealed container for his own remaining days.

One evening, the phone call came.

His condition had flared. He had been taken to the hospital — agitated, disoriented, frightening the staff in a way that was not who he was, but who the fear inside him had briefly turned him into. When the body is that overwhelmed and has that little language for it, distress becomes noise. It becomes force. And the world, which had never been especially patient with him, became less so.

He was admitted for observation. Then he was moved. Then, when he had stabilised enough to be discharged, the facility where he had been living informed the family that they would not take him back.

His daughter called me.

I had met her only once, briefly. A woman in her forties, careful voice, the controlled breathing of a person who had been holding a difficult family situation together for longer than was reasonable. On the phone that night, something in her voice had come undone.

I don't know where to take him, she said. They keep telling me there isn't a place.

I did not deliberate. I did not run a risk calculation. Something in me answered before the thinking mind arrived.

Bring him to us.

When he arrived, he was not the man I had been visiting.

The hospitalisation had taken something out of him. He was thinner. More watchful. The softness that had begun, over those weeks of sitting by the window, to come back into his face — that softness had withdrawn again. A body that had started to trust the world had been reminded, once more, that trust was a risk it could not yet afford.

We did not push him.

We simply let him be there. We let the room be quiet. We let the staff move through their day without making him the event at the center of it. We let ordinary life continue around him, and we waited — not for him to settle, but for him to decide, in his own time, that settling was safe.

It took weeks.

And then, one afternoon, I walked past his room and found him standing at the window.

He had not stood at a window on his own in a long time.

He turned when he heard me. He did not say anything. He simply held my eye for a moment, and I understood.

Something was coming back.

There is a moment I have thought about many times since. I want to tell you about it honestly, because it has no drama in it, and drama is not where the real thing lives.

It was an ordinary afternoon. I had a few hours free. I asked him if he would like to go outside.

He looked at me the way a person looks when they have stopped expecting invitations.

We walked out through the side door. The air was cold — early spring, the kind of cold that still remembers winter but is no longer committed to it. He stopped just outside the door and stood for a long moment, breathing.

Just breathing.

I realized, standing next to him, that I did not know the last time he had stood outside without a purpose. Without being moved from one building to another. Without being wheeled, or accompanied, or managed.

Just standing in the air, because the air was there and he was there and nothing in particular was required of either of them.

We walked slowly across the lawn. Not far. His body did not carry him far. But far enough.

At the edge of the lawn there was a small patch of turned earth where someone had started a vegetable bed the previous season and then abandoned it. Weeds had come in. The soil was rough, compacted, waiting for someone to remember it.

He stopped beside it.

He looked at it for a long time.

Then he knelt — slowly, carefully, in the way a body kneels when kneeling is no longer automatic — and he put his hand flat against the dirt.

He did not say anything.

He kept his hand there.

I stood behind him, and I watched a man return to himself through the palm of his hand.

He lived with us longer than anyone had expected.

In that time, something happened that I do not know how to describe precisely, only how to witness. He became softer. Not weaker — softer. The vigilance in him lowered by degrees. He began to initiate things — small things, the scale of things a person initiates when they are first testing whether initiative is permitted. A word at breakfast. A preference about where to sit. A request, once, for a specific kind of soup he remembered from childhood.

His daughter came often. Other family members, too. The conversations between them were not the brittle, managed exchanges of a family organized around a problem. They were the conversations of a family remembering how to be ordinary together.

He never gardened a full row of tomatoes again. His body would not allow it.

But he weeded that small patch of earth with his hands, on afternoons when the weather permitted, for as long as he was able. He did not speak much while he worked. He did not need to. The work was itself the speech.

I would watch him sometimes from the window, and I would think:

This is what the valve opening looks like.

Not catharsis. Not a dramatic awakening. A man kneeling in the dirt on a Tuesday afternoon, doing something the world had stopped allowing him to do, and being returned — one slow handful of earth at a time — to himself.

His daughter came to see him often in those months. One afternoon, as I was leaving, she followed me into the hallway. She stopped me there. She said something I have carried with me since.

She said, *Thank you for letting him be a person again.*

I did not know what to say. I still don't.

I simply know that the sentence was not about me. It was about what becomes possible when one human being refuses to let another human being disappear into a file.

There is a question that sits underneath every act of real care, and most of us never ask it.

Not, "What is wrong with this person?"

But, "What have they not been allowed to be?"

He taught me that. Without meaning to. Without, I think, ever knowing he was teaching anything.

He simply lived what he had left to live in the presence of people who would not make him smaller than he was. And in that presence, something opened in him that had been closed for a very long time.

And something, I will tell you honestly, opened in me.

Because you do not sit with a person returning to himself and remain unchanged. The opening is not contained in the one who opens. It moves through the room. It moves through the people watching. It becomes part of you — quietly, without ceremony, in a way you will only recognize later, in some unrelated moment, when you find yourself acting from a clarity you did not have before.

That is what an open valve does in the world. It does not announce itself. It simply acts from what it knows. And the action is right because nothing in the way distorted it.

He was not cured. His body remained his body. His circumstances remained, to the end, the circumstances of a man who had aged past what the world knew how to hold.

But he was known. He was not a problem being managed. He was a person being accompanied.

And in the end, that is what remained — not the placements, not the files, not the institutional decisions made about him by people who had never sat in the room long enough to see him.

What remained was a small patch of turned earth at the edge of a lawn, and the memory of a hand, flat against the dirt, on an afternoon when a man came home to himself.

That is what an open valve sounds like.

Not a technique. Not a philosophy.

A human being, open enough to act from what they knew — and a life, changed by it, however briefly.

That is the legacy.

Not what is achieved.

What is felt, in the presence of someone whose valve is open.

What remains.

31

The Valve Opens

We began with a man sitting in a room where everyone had already decided what he was.

We began with the moment someone finally sat down and listened.

With a quiet sentence that landed like a stone in still water:

"I haven't touched dirt in six years."

That was not a complaint. It was a recognition. A body signalling to another body: I know what I used to be. I know what has been taken. Please do not leave without hearing it.

What he needed was not expertise. He needed presence. He needed someone to arrive without a predetermined conclusion and remain long enough for the nervous system to stop guarding itself.

When that finally happened, something opened.

Not because of technique. Not because of insight. Because the body, in the presence of genuine safety, does what the body has always wanted to do.

It opens.

The valve is not a flaw. It was never a flaw.

It is the body's most faithful act of love toward itself. Every tightening was an attempt to survive something that felt unsurvivable. Every closing was a promise: not now, but not never. We will feel this when it is safe. We will open when we are ready. We will return to ourselves when the world finally allows it.

You were not damaged by what closed you. You were cared for by it.

What this book has tried to offer is a new environment. One in which the nervous system can begin to receive the message it has been waiting for: it is safe now. You can open. Not all at once. Not on a schedule someone else set. But in rhythm with what feels true, at the pace your own body sets, in the direction your own intelligence points.

That intelligence is not separate from love. It is love, moving without obstruction. Seeing clearly. Acting from that seeing. Not effortfully. Because nothing is in the way.

The world does not need more people performing wholeness.

It needs more people actually inhabiting themselves.

An open valve changes the quality of everything it touches. The conversations you have. The way you listen. The capacity to be moved without being swept away.

You become easier to love and harder to control.

You become someone who knows the difference between a boundary and a wall.

You become someone whose presence is itself a kind of safety — because the nervous system is contagious, and an open valve invites other valves to open.

In families: the inheritance ends here. Your children feel, in your presence, that they are allowed to be themselves. That their feelings do not need to be hidden to keep the peace. That the valve does not have to close in this house.

In friendship: the kind of conversation both people remember for years. Not because anything dramatic was said — because something true was. Because for an hour, neither person performed, and what was real between them was finally allowed to speak.

This is the legacy. Not what is built or achieved. The quality of what others feel in your presence. That is what remains.

There is nothing to fix.

There is only the slow, trustworthy, entirely human work of returning to yourself. Not to a better version. Not to the version you imagined you should have been. To the one who is already here — the one who survived everything and is still, quietly, wanting to live fully.

Set this book down for a moment.

Feel the weight of it leaving your hands.

Notice what is here. The quality of the room. The pace of your breath. Whatever has shifted — or hasn't — in the time you've been reading.

You do not have to name it. You do not have to understand it. You do not have to become anything different from what you are right now, in this moment, sitting with whatever this has stirred.

The valve does not open all at once. It opens the way spring arrives — not in a single day, but in a hundred small unremarkable ones, until one morning you notice that something is different. That the air has changed. That the holding has softened, just slightly, and you are not sure exactly when it did.

That morning is not far from here.

It may, in fact, already have begun.

The valve opens.

Life flows.

The body knows it is safe.

And it always was.

— *W. G. Vale*

CODA

The Door Is Not the Room

I want to say one last thing about the valve — the thing that matters most, and the thing that is easiest to miss.

The valve is not the truth of this book.

It is a doorway to the truth. And the two are not the same.

— — —

I have come to see, slowly, that the most useful teachings carry inside them the seed of their own dissolution. They are built to be outgrown. The valve is one of these.

It served you, perhaps, because abstract instruction could not reach where you actually live. "Be present." "Be aware." "Let go." These are true, and for many people they are also useless — because the mind hears the instruction and immediately turns it into a task. Another thing to get right. Another way to fail.

The valve gave you somewhere to begin that was not abstract. A tight chest. A held breath. A jaw that would not release. The body, honest as always, showing you exactly where the holding lives.

That was the doorway.

What the doorway opens onto is something simpler than the door itself — and, in the end, more important.

— — —

There is a risk, once the valve has helped you, of the valve becoming another identity. Another thing to monitor. Another project.

I am working on my valve.

My valve is closing again.

Why won't my valve open?

If you find yourself living this way — relating to yourself through the metaphor, year after year — then the metaphor has outlived its usefulness. The scaffold has begun to look like the building.

Set it down.

— — —

What the valve was always pointing toward is something that cannot, in the end, be named without distortion. Other teachers have tried. They have called it presence. Awareness. The witness. The one who sees. Ram Dass pointed at it by pointing at love. Krishnamurti pointed at it by refusing, again and again, to let his listeners turn it into a technique. Hawkins mapped it. Tolle named it. Maharaj-ji, characteristically, simply laughed.

I will not add another name to the pile.

I will only say this: there is something in you that sees the valve. That something is not the valve. It is what the valve was always trying to return you to.

And it was never absent. It could not have been absent. It is what has been reading these pages.

— — —

The valve is the finger.

Awareness is the moon.

Please do not spend your life studying the finger.

— — —

The practice, in the end, is almost embarrassingly simple.

Notice that you are holding. That is the valve. It is useful. It will always be useful, in the moments when noticing the body is the clearest doorway available.

Then — and this is the turn most people miss do not make a project of opening. Do not work on the valve. Do not try to be more present, more aware, more free.

Simply rest your attention on what is here, without agenda.

That resting is the whole thing.

The body, feeling itself finally met rather than worked on, releases in its own time. Not because you released it. Because you stopped preventing it.

— — —

I want to offer you three sentences. They are the entire practice, compressed small enough to carry.

"I notice I am holding."

This is the valve. The body, seen.

"I am not trying to fix it."

This is the turn. The hand releasing the project.

"I am simply here with it."

This is awareness. Nothing more is required.

— — —

You do not need to graduate from the valve. You do not need to abandon it. Use it as long as it helps — and it will help, for many ordinary days, for many ordinary years.

But know, underneath the using, what it was always for.

It was for the moment you stop needing it. The moment you notice that what has been doing the noticing all along is the thing you were actually looking for.

That moment is not a destination. It is already here. It has been here on every page of this book. It is here now, reading these words, aware of the body in the chair, aware of the breath, aware of whatever is rising or quieting in you as you read.

That is the whole of it.

The valve opens. The door opens. And then, quietly — because this is how these things actually work — the door itself dissolves, and you find that you were always already in the room.

— — —

There is nothing to fix.

There is nothing to open.

There is only what has been here all along, waiting quietly to be noticed.

— W. G. V.

On Whose Shoulders

I did not discover the valve. I found it, in myself and in the rooms I sat in, after decades of work by people far more rigorous than I am. This book does not cite them on every page, because the book is a companion, not a textbook. But it would be wrong to close without naming them.

If these pages have moved you, and if you want to go further into the science of what I have described here, begin with the following. Each of them has written a book that changed how a generation of clinicians understands the body.

Candace Pert. The neuroscientist who proved, at the level of the cell, what mystics had been saying for centuries — that emotion is not confined to the brain but is chemically distributed throughout the body. Her work on neuropeptide receptors gave us a vocabulary for what the body had always been doing. Her book, Molecules of Emotion, is where the modern conversation begins.

Bessel van der Kolk. The psychiatrist who has spent a lifetime documenting how the body stores what the mind cannot bear. The Body Keeps the Score is the book most often placed in my hands by patients who have been trying to explain, for years, what they feel in their tissue.

Stephen Porges. The scientist whose polyvagal theory describes, with precision, the branches of the nervous system that govern safety, connection, and shutdown. If you have ever felt yourself freeze without knowing why, his work explains the machinery beneath the feeling.

Gabor Maté. The physician who has shown, case by case, how illness often begins as unheard emotion and unmet need. His work reminds us that the body is not the site of the problem. It is the site of the message.

Peter Levine. The psychologist whose somatic work, Waking the Tiger and In an Unspoken Voice, gave us a practice for completing the responses the body was never permitted to finish. He is, in many ways, the founder of the field these pages walk through.

I have also been shaped, in ways too deep to footnote, by the spiritual teachers who understood the valve long before the research caught up: Krishnamurti, Ram Dass, Neem Karoli Baba, and the quiet tradition of sitting with what is.

This book stands on all of their shoulders. I offer it not as a replacement for their work, but as a bridge — for the reader who may come to the science later, or not at all, but who needs, first, a companion on the path.

The valve opens when it opens. They helped me understand why.

Acknowledgments

This book would not exist without the people who taught me what it means to feel safe enough to open.

To the man who first taught me that a person is not a case file — I carry what you taught me on every page. You know who you are, and the people who loved you know.

To every person I have had the privilege of sitting with, in the ordinary rooms where real things happen: thank you for trusting me with what you were holding. It changed how I understand my own.

To the ones whose stories taught me that the most meaningful healing rarely arrives as rescue — that it arrives, instead, as presence. As someone staying in the room long enough that a life can come back into focus. You know who you are, and the ones of you who have passed know too, wherever presence continues.

To the readers, the practitioners, and everyone carrying something they have not yet found words for: this book was written for you. May you find in these pages something of what you have been waiting to receive.

To my wife, whose presence has been my steadiest container: thank you for the mirror, and for staying when what was reflected was difficult.

And to the body itself — patient, faithful, never truly closed.

Only waiting.

— *W. G. V.*

You have been carrying this for a long time.

You can set it down now.

Not all of it. Not today.

But some of it.

Enough.

About This Book

A Note on Privacy

The stories in this book are composites. Names, identifying details, medical histories, family structures, locations, and circumstances have been changed or fictionalized. Any resemblance to a specific living or deceased person is unintentional. What is preserved is emotional truth, not biographical fact.

Disclaimer

This book is intended for educational and inspirational purposes only. It is not a substitute for professional medical or psychological advice. Always seek guidance from a qualified professional regarding your health.

Copyright

For permission requests, contact: info@vibranteverymoment.com

The Valve™ is a trademark of W. G. Vale.

ISBN (Paperback): 979-8-9956828-1-3

First Edition, 2026

Published by Vale Press

www.ingramcontent.com/pod-product-compliance
Lightning Source LLC
LaVergne TN
LVHW010840120826
845149LV00017B/3327